NUMMER STORIEN

THE NUMBER STORY

SMALL BOOK ONE

ENGLISH - DANISH

Numbers Teach Children
Their Number Names

written and illustrated by

MISS ANNA

Early Reader Edition of *The Number Story 1*
Bronze Medal Winner, 2016 Wishing Shelf Book Award

Cover by | Lumpy Publishing
Layout by | Lumpy Publishing
Translated by Nora Liam
Coloring by Jieeun Woo and Maria Mirabella

Library of Congress Control Number: 2018902040

Names: Miss Anna, author.
Title: Number story : numbers teach children their number names / Miss Anna.
Description: Portland, OR: Lumpy Publishing, 2018.
Identifiers: ISBN 978-1-945977-27-5 | LCCN 2018902040
Summary: The pictures and rhymes present stories which introduce numbers 0-10.
Subjects: LCSH Numeration—English--Danish--Pictorial works--Juvenile literature. | BISAC JUVENILE NONFICTION /
Languages: English--Danish
Classification: LCC QA141.3 .M57 2018 | DDC 513—dc23

Publisher: Lumpy Publishing
Website: www.missannabooks.com
Email: missanna@missannabooks.com

Paperback: ISBN 978-1-945977-27-5
Printed in the U.S.A.   1 3 5 7 9 10 8 6 4 2

Vil du lære
vores navne?

It is very easy and a lot of fun!

Det er meget let og en masse sjov!

Say-along our little jingle

Sig-langs vores lille *jingle*

starting from Number One!

Startende fra nummer et!

1

ONE looks like my one finger.

EN

ser ud til min ene finger.

1
ONE!
EN!

2

TWO   trails a tail.

TO

har en halen.

A TAIL!   EN HALE!

3

THREE has bumps.

TRE

har kurver.

BUMPY! KURVET!

4

FOUR carries a sail.

FIRE

bærer et sejl.

A SAIL!
EN SAIL!

5

FIVE   is a racing track.

FEM

er en racerbane.

VROOM
BRUMM!
1

SIX   curves like a snail.

SEKS

kurver som en snegl.

A SNAIL! EN SNEGL!

7
SEVEN has a sharp angle.
SYV
har en skarp vinkel.

OUCH!
AV!

8

EIGHT is rollercoaster rails.

OTTE

er en rutsjebane.

YIPPEE!

NINE is a bubble on a stick.

NI

er en boble på en pind.

A BUBBLE! EN BOBLE!

10

TEN   is an eye of a whale.

TI

er det ene øje af en hval.

WINK!
BLINKE!

And
OG

0

ZERO is an empty pail.

NUL

er en tom spand.

IT'S EMPTY!
DEN ER TOM!

Thank you for playing with us today.

We had a lot of fun too!

Tak for at spille med os i dag.

Vi havde også meget sjov!

We are your Number friends,
Zero to Ten,
Who will be here for you~
Vi er dit nummer venner,
Zero til Ti,
Hvem vil være her for dig~

Bye-bye now!
See you again soon!
Farvel nu!
Se dig igen snart!

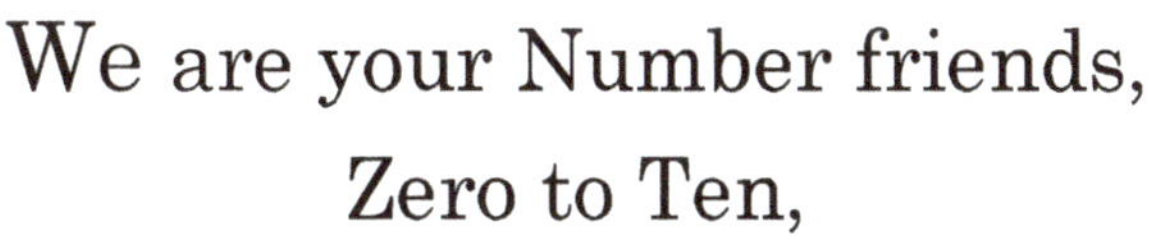

The Numbers are *SINGING* too!

To sing-a-long, look for Miss Anna Number Story
at your favorite music store like iTUNES.

MP3

Numbers 0-10
IDENTIFYING & COUNTING

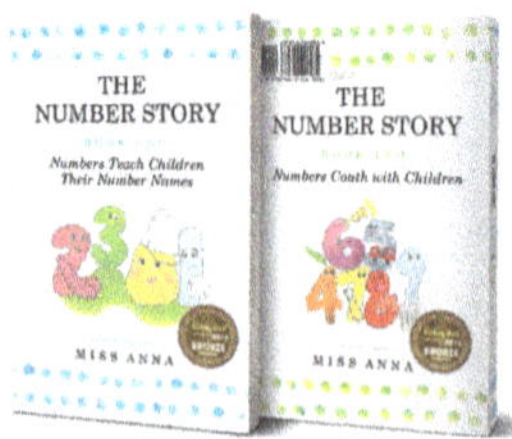

Number Story 1 & 2

isbn: 978-0-996216-48-7

Numbers 11-20 & Ordinals
first, second, third...

Number Story 3 & 4

isbn: 978-1-945977-01-5

Numbers 0-100 & Place Values
ones, tens, hundreds...

Number Story 5 & 6

isbn: 978-1-945977-06-0

About Clocks & Telling Time
hours, minutes, seconds...

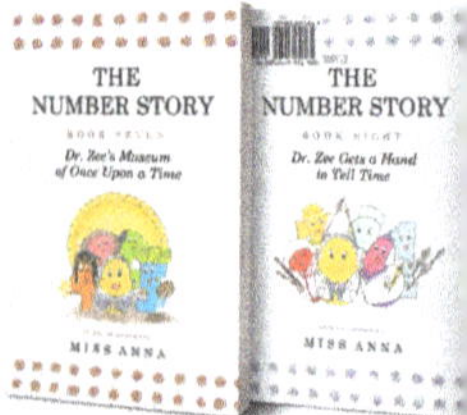

Number Story 7 & 8

isbn: 978-1-949320-40-

For more Miss Anna books to love,
visit us at

www.missannabooks.com

Numbers are working hard all over the world!
Come Travel the World with Us!